Please visit our website, www.garethstevens.com. For a free color catalog of all our high-quality books, call toll free 1-800-542-2595 or fax 1-877-542-2596.

Cataloging-in-Publication Data
Names: Rajczak Nelson, Kristen, author.
Title: Simu Liu is Shang-Chi / Kristen Rajczak Nelson.
Description: Buffalo, New York : Gareth Stevens Publishing, 2023. | Series: The human behind the hero | Includes bibliographic references index.
Identifiers: LCCN 2022022154 (print) | LCCN 2022022155 (ebook) | ISBN 9781538283899 (library binding) | ISBN 9781538283875 (paperback) | ISBN 9781538283905 (ebook)
Subjects: LCSH: Liu, Simu, 1989—Juvenile literature. | Motion picture actors and actresses–Canada–Biography–Juvenile literature. | Shang-Chi (Fictitious character)–Juvenile literature. | LCGFT: Biographies.
Classification: LCC PN2308.L58 R35 2023 (print) | LCC PN2308.L58 (ebook) | DDC 791.4302/8092 [B]–dc23/eng/20220517
LC record available at https://lccn.loc.gov/2022022154
LC ebook record available at https://lccn.loc.gov/2022022155

First Edition

Published in 2023 by
Gareth Stevens Publishing
2544 Clinton St
Buffalo, NY 14224

Copyright © 2023 Gareth Stevens Publishing

Designer: Rachel Rising
Editor: Kristen Rajczak Nelson

Photo credits: Cover, pp. 1, 15 Eugene Powers/Shutterstock.com; pp. 1-32 KID_A/Shutterstock.com; pp. 1-32 gn8/Shutterstock.com; pp. 5, 9 Tinseltown/Shutterstock.com; p. 7 Content zilla/Shutterstock.com; p. 11 https://commons.wikimedia.org/wiki/File:SLiuRedCarpet.jpg; p. 13 https://commons.wikimedia.org/wiki/File:Simu_Liu_on_The_Beaverton.jpg; p. 17 Shawn Goldberg/Shutterstock.com; p. 19 https://commons.wikimedia.org/wiki/File:Simu_Liu_(48469091851).jpg; p. 21 Alpha Photo / Alamy Stock Photo; p. 23 Album / Alamy Stock Photo; p. 25 DFree/Shutterstock.com; p. 27 PictureLux / The Hollywood Archive / Alamy Stock Photo; p. 29 ZUMA Press, Inc. / Alamy Stock Photo.

CPSIA compliance information: Batch #CW23GS. For further information contact Gareth Stevens at 1-800-542-2595.

CONTENTS

BORN ABROAD

Simu Liu was born on April 19, 1989. His family lived in Harbin, a city in northeast China. Not long after Simu was born, his parents moved to Canada to go to school. He stayed in China with his grandparents.

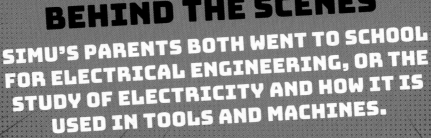

BEHIND THE SCENES

SIMU'S PARENTS BOTH WENT TO SCHOOL FOR ELECTRICAL ENGINEERING, OR THE STUDY OF ELECTRICITY AND HOW IT IS USED IN TOOLS AND MACHINES.

A BIG MOVE

Simu moved to Canada to live with his parents in 1995. He didn't get along with his parents when he was growing up in Mississauga, Ontario. Simu felt they didn't understand the Canadian **culture** he was becoming a part of.

MISSISSAUGA, ONTARIO

BEHIND THE SCENES

SIMU WAS FIVE YEARS OLD WHEN HIS DAD TOOK HIM TO CANADA. HE FELT LIKE HE WAS MEETING HIS PARENTS FOR THE FIRST TIME.

UNDER PRESSURE

Simu's parents pushed him to do well in school. It paid off. He went to the University of Western Ontario. He became an **accountant**. But he wasn't happy. Simu said this showed in his work. He wasn't a very good accountant!

JACKIE CHAN

BEHIND THE SCENES

WHEN SIMU WAS YOUNG, HE SAID THE ONLY ASIAN ACTORS HE SAW WERE JACKIE CHAN AND JET LI: "I THINK THE CHARACTERS THAT THEY WERE FORCED TO PLAY WERE ALSO VERY EXAGGERATED *VERSIONS* OF WHAT ASIAN PEOPLE ACTUALLY ARE."

In 2012, Simu was fired from, or asked to leave, his job. Simu worried about telling his parents. He worried even more about telling them he might want to be an actor—not an accountant!

BEHIND THE SCENES

AS AN ADULT, SIMU LIVED IN TORONTO, CANADA, ONE OF THE LARGEST CITIES IN NORTH AMERICA.

EXTRA, EXTRA!

Simu's first real acting job was as an extra, or background person, in the movie *Pacific Rim.* He had to be painted blue! The job made him "totally fall in love with the magic of movies." After that, he took any acting job he could.

BEHIND THE SCENES

ONE OF SIMU'S EARLY ACTING JOBS WAS
DRESSING UP AS SPIDER-MAN FOR
BIRTHDAY PARTIES!

13

Simu worked hard for a few years to break into acting. He did some **stunt** work in Toronto. He was only an extra or had very small parts in TV shows and movies. Simu didn't have much money—but he kept at it!

BEHIND THE SCENES

SIMU ONLY TOLD HIS PARENTS HE WAS ACTING BECAUSE HE WAS GOING TO BE IN A NATIONAL COMMERCIAL, OR TV AD, IN CANADA, AND THEY WERE LIKELY TO SEE IT!

REPRESENT!

Finally, Simu got a part on *Kim's Convenience*. The TV show started airing in Canada in 2016. Simu plays Jung Kim, part of a Korean Canadian family that runs a store. Simu felt the show was important for Asian **representation**.

CAST OF *KIM'S CONVENIENCE*

BEHIND THE SCENES

SIMU THOUGHT THE WRITERS OF *KIM'S CONVENIENCE* NEEDED MORE INPUT FROM THOSE WHO KNEW WHAT IT WAS LIKE TO BE AN ASIAN **IMMIGRANT.** STILL, THE SHOW RAN UNTIL 2021.

In 2019, Simu learned he would help bring more representation to a bigger platform: the Marvel Cinematic Universe (MCU). He was chosen to play Shang-Chi! He did a back flip when he tried out for the part.

BEHIND THE SCENES

THE MCU IS THE SHARED UNIVERSE OF MANY SUPERHERO MOVIES (AND SOME TV SHOWS) BASED ON CHARACTERS FROM MARVEL COMICS.

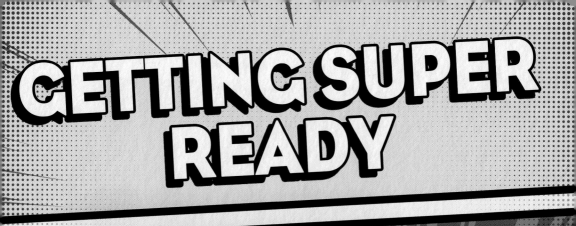

GETTING SUPER READY

Simu knew some stunts and was pretty fit. But for *Shang-Chi and the Legend of the Ten Rings*, he had to look and move like a superhero! Simu had to do a lot of stretching, or moving his body in a way to make it more bendable.

BEHIND THE SCENES

SHANG-CHI FIRST APPEARED IN MARVEL COMICS IN 1973. THE ORIGINAL STORIES INCLUDED MANY ASIAN **STEREOTYPES** THAT SIMU AND THE MARVEL TEAM AIMED TO LEAVE OUT OF THE MOVIE.

21

Shang-Chi is a master martial artist. To play him, Simu trained to fight on screen. He got hurt filming some of these fights! Simu had to prepare for fame too. Fans were very excited for Shang-Chi to join the MCU.

BEHIND THE SCENES

MARTIAL ARTS ARE WAYS THAT PEOPLE TRAIN TO FIGHT OR MOVE THAT OFTEN COME FROM ASIAN CULTURES. THEY INCLUDE KARATE, JIUJITSU, AND TAE KWON DO, AMONG OTHERS.

MEANINGFUL WORK

Simu would be playing the first Asian superhero to lead a movie in the MCU. This meant a lot to him: "This is all I wanted as a kid, as a 6-year-old, maybe even as a 16-year-old, if I'm honest."

BEHIND THE SCENES

THE DIRECTOR AND TWO OF THE WRITERS OF *SHANG-CHI AND THE LEGEND OF THE TEN RINGS* WERE ALSO ASIAN AMERICAN.

In 2021, *Shang-Chi and the Legend of the Ten Rings* came out. It was one of the most successful movies of the year! Fans loved the movie's action and the funny moments between Simu and costar Awkwafina.

BEHIND THE SCENES

WITH HIS NEW FAME, SIMU BEGAN TO SPEAK OUT MORE ABOUT ASIAN REPRESENTATION AND STEREOTYPES, AMONG OTHER TOPICS.

FUTURE PLANS

Simu will play Shang-Chi again. But he wants to be in all different kinds of movies! He said: "We need to show Asian Americans in ... all sorts of light. So that will be what the next few steps of my **career** are focused on."

BEHIND THE SCENES

SIMU WROTE A BOOK CALLED WE WERE DREAMERS: AN IMMIGRANT SUPERHERO ORIGIN STORY. IT'S ABOUT HIS LIFE AS A CHINESE IMMIGRANT AND BECOMING AN ACTOR. IT CAME OUT IN 2022.

TIMELINE

1989 SIMU LIU IS BORN ON APRIL 19 IN HARBIN, CHINA.

1995 HE MOVES TO CANADA.

2011 SIMU FINISHES SCHOOL AT THE UNIVERSITY OF WESTERN ONTARIO. HE STARTS WORKING AS AN ACCOUNTANT.

2012 HE IS FIRED FROM HIS JOB AS AN ACCOUNTANT. HE IS AN EXTRA IN *PACIFIC RIM*.

2016 SIMU BEGINS STARRING IN *KIM'S CONVENIENCE*.

2019 HE IS CHOSEN TO PLAY SHANG-CHI.

2021 *SHANG-CHI AND THE LEGEND OF THE TEN RINGS* COMES OUT.

2022 SIMU'S BOOK, *WE WERE DREAMERS: AN IMMIGRANT SUPERHERO ORIGIN STORY*, COMES OUT.

FOR MORE INFORMATION

BOOKS

Chen, Michael. *Shang-Chi.* New York, NY: Little Golden Books, an imprint of Random House Children's Books, 2021.

Glass, Calliope, et al. *5-Minute Marvel Stories.* Los Angeles, CA: Marvel, 2022.

WEBSITES

Shang-Chi | Characters | Marvel
www.marvel.com/characters/shang-chi
Find out more about Shang-Chi in the movie and in the comics!

Simu Liu - IMDb
www.imdb.com/name/nm4855517/
Follow along with Simu's career on the Internet Movie Database.

GLOSSARY

accountant: Someone whose job is to keep records about the money that a business or person has.

career: The job someone chooses to do for a long time.

culture: The beliefs and ways of life of a group of people.

immigrant: One who comes to a country to settle there.

representation: The way a TV show, movie, book, or other media deals with and presents age, gender, or ethnicity.

stereotype: An often unfair and untrue belief people have about all members of a certain group.

stunt: A hard or dangerous action done for a movie or TV show.

version: A form of something that is different from others.

INDEX